How sleepy are you?

Do you feel like whining and
rubbing your eyes?

small world

Bedtime!

Gwenyth Swain

ZERO TO TEN

To find out more about the pictures in this book, turn to page 22.
To find out more about sharing this book with children, turn to page 24.

The photographs in this book are reproduced with the permission of: © Trip/R. Chester, front cover; © Jack Ballard/Visuals Unlimited, Inc., back cover; © Dermot Tatlow/Panos Pictures, p.1; © Jennie Woodcock/Reflections Photolibrary/CORBIS, p.3; © Earl and Nazima Kowall/CORBIS, p.4; © Trip/H. Rogers, pp. 5, 15, 17; © Jeff Greenberg/Visuals Unlimited, Inc., p.6; © Betty Press/Panos Pictures, p.7; © Mark E. Gibson/Visuals Unlimited, Inc., p.8; Robert Van der Hilst/CORBIS, p.9; © Jodi Jacobson/Peter Arnold, Inc., p.10; © Trip/D. Houghton, p.11; © Sean Sprague/Panos Pictures, p.12; © Owen Franken/CORBIS, p.13; © Jeremy Hartley/Panos Pictures, p.14; © Alison Wright/CORBIS, p.16; © Trip/S.Grant, p.18; © Giacomo Pirozzi/Panos Pictures, p.19; © Dean Chapman/Panos Pictures, p.20; © Deutsch/Sprague/Panos Pictures, p.21.

First published in this edition in Great Britain 2005 by Zero To Ten Limited, part of the Evans Publishing Group, 2A Portman Mansions, Chiltern St, London W1U 6NR

Published by arrangement with Carolrhoda Books, Inc., a division of Lerner Publishing Group, 241 First Avenue North, Minneapolis, MN 55401, U.S.A.

A CIP catalogue record for this book is available from the British Library.

ISBN 1 84089 393 1

Printed in China by WKT

Have you been up so long,
you can't help but cry?

Take a nap in a lap.

Rest your head on a camp bed.

Snooze on an airplane up high in the air.

Sleepyheads can sleep almost anywhere!

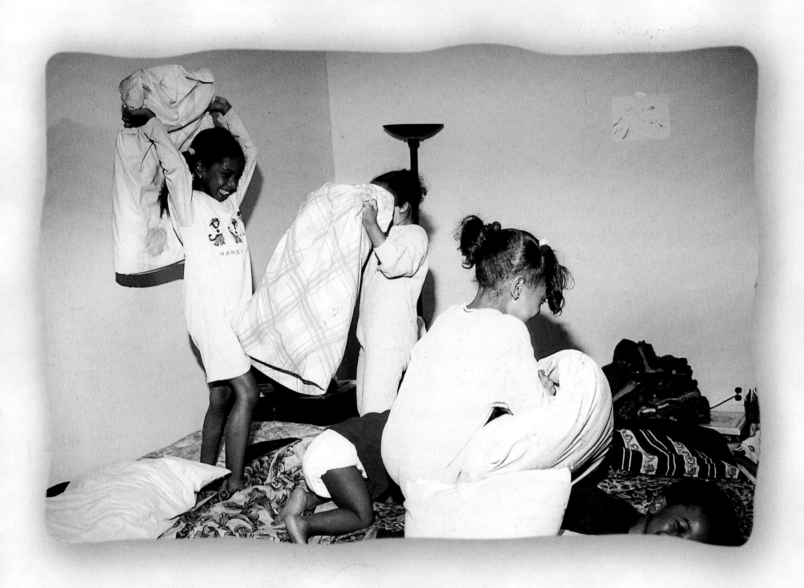

Do you get much rest away from home?

Do you sleep best when you're not alone?

Brush your teeth before you hit the sheets.

Put on pyjamas. Cover your feet.

Give thanks. Say good night.

Don't forget to turn out the light.

Dream up in a hammock.
Sleep down on the ground.

Find the warmest, softest pillow around.

Tuck yourself in till you feel snug.

Ask someone for a goodnight hug.

Lie close, warm and safe.

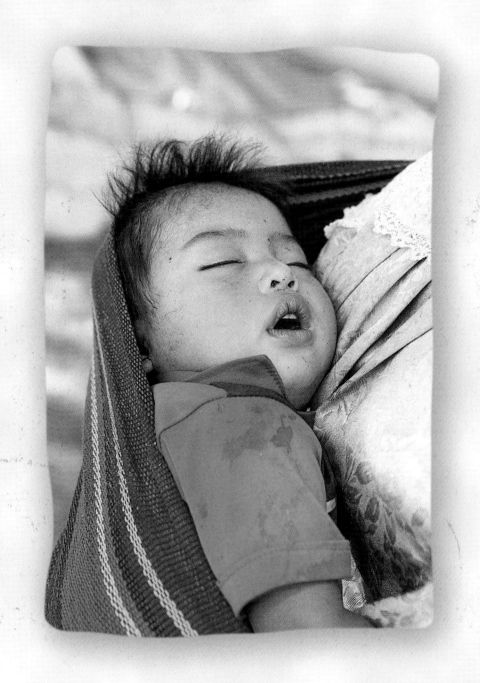

Naptime is the best time, anytime, anyplace!

More about the Pictures

Front cover: A girl in Britain reads on into the night, even after the lights are out!

Back cover: A Korean boy naps during a boat trip.

Page 1: Some tiny spectators just can't stay awake while their parents watch opera in Tibet.

Page 3: A tired baby rubs her eyes in Britain.

Page 4: A mother in India holds on to her sleep son.

Page 5: Sometimes when we're tired all we can think to do is cry.

Page 6: A child takes a nap on her father's lap in Florida, USA.

Page 7: It's nap time at a nursery in Trinidad, Cuba.

Page 8: A young girl snoozes while a jet whisks her through the air, travelling at hundreds of kilometres per hour.

Page 9: In Kuqa, China, a little boy falls asleep in a carpet shop.

Page 10: Sometimes it's hard to get sleepy, especially during a pillow fight.

 *Page 11:* This girl sleeps best when she's cuddling her Siamese cat.

 *Page 12:* In Prague in the Czech Republic, a boy brushes his teeth before bed.

 *Page 13:* A boy in Paris, France, sits snug in pyjamas and looks at a book.

 *Page 14:* It's bedtime for these children in Turkmenistan in central Asia.

 *Page 15:* A girl in Britain reads on into the night, even after the lights are out!

 *Page 16:* In the Amazon River area of Peru, a baby rocks in a hammock.

 *Page 17:* A British girl holds on to her pillow. Do you have a favourite soft pillow?

 *Page 18:* A boy reads to his cousin tucked in a spare bed. This spare bed is low and rolls under a higher bed when not being used.

 *Page 19:* A mother hugs her sick son, who must stay the night at a children's hospital in Iraq.

 *Page 20:* This young girl lies close to her brother in Thailand.

 *Page 21:* Safe in a sling, this baby in Guatemala can sleep anytime, anyplace.

A Note to Adults on Sharing This Book

Help your child to become a lifelong reader. Read this book together, taking turns as you both read out loud. Look over the photographs and choose your favourites. Sound out new words and go back to them later to look at them again. Then try these 'extensions' – activities that extend the experience of reading and build discussion and problem-solving skills.

Talk about Bedtime
All around the world, people enjoy their rest. This book shows children asleep or getting ready for bed in many different countries and cultures. Ask your child to describe his or her bedtime routines. How do the bedtime routines shown in this book differ from those of your child? How are they the same?

Sleep in Different Ways
With your child, choose a new bedtime habit that you want to try. It can be as simple as singing a song or reading a story before going to bed. Or try these ideas: borrow a hammock and try it out for a nap. Dig out a sleeping bag and have an indoor camping trip. Which way of sleeping seemed easier or harder? Warmer or cooler?